California MBE Questions, Answers and Analysis (1)

authored by

Value Bar Prep books

For
CaliforniaBarHelp.com

Home of legal celebrities and superstars.

Thank you for buying this material and congratulations on your projected success. The questions are structured the same way as multi-state bar examination (MBE). The subject areas covered are Property Contracts Criminal Law and procedure Evidence Torts and Constitutional law.

Although the NCBE says that 10 of its 200 examination questions are not scored but are merely being tested for possible inclusion on future examinations, this volume of the material has 100 questions and the second volume has another 100 questions for a total of 200 success-oriented questions and answers.

Bonus questions are also featured, all along with analysis.

Success on the MBE depends on close familiarity with all elements of the law in a given subject area. Mastery of the legal principles is key. Such mastery is achieved through intelligent study.

It's suggested here that during the last 3 or 4 months of serious revision before the examination, two complete weeks should be spent revising each subject exclusively.

For illustration a student may spend
March 1 - March 14 on Constitutional law.
March 8 - 22 on Torts.
March 16 - 30 on Evidence and so on.

This involves studying capsule summaries, short outlines, any classroom notes, audio tapes and flashcards.

Flashcards are available both free and for sale on the internet.

The bulk of the student's heavy reading such as any hornbooks should have been done during the various semesters. The last few months before the examination should be mostly dedicated to focused revision of such things as issue spotting aids, outlines and quality summaries.

It's a good MBE strategy to set a goal for how many questions the student will answer correctly. That goal may be 140 (which is said to be the average on many state bar examinations), 145, 150, 160 or even 170 or 180.

Having set the goal it must be pursued. That is where materials like this one come in useful.

Many profs instruct candidates that it is necessary to attempt 1 to 3 thousand MBEs before sitting for the test.

This advice is well founded because on examination day a candidate who has attempted that many likely won't find a lot of unfamiliar issues or questions.

If you're unable to acquire that many test questions however, it's been found to be a good strategy to answer and re-answer the questions the candidate does have, over and over again: the same ones.

The advantage is that by the time the candidate has attempted the same questions many times - even after getting them right on a number of previous occasions - common fact patterns and even hidden issues raised in them become set in the candidate's mind just as firmly as if the applicant had bought thousands of questions.

The effect is that even if on the examination

an issue is tested with a different fact pattern, the candidate will recognize the issue and probably answer correctly.

Therefore, the candidate should remain encouraged even if they don't have access to thousands of practice questions, which can be expensive. A few hundred attempted over and over will still likely cover the majority of the actual examination. The familiarity that will come from such necessary repetition will make success likely. The National conference of bar examiners is the organization that handles the MBE for a lot of jurisdictions. It has a website at www.ncbex.org.

That site has MBE information that will be relevant to most bar candidates across the country including those in California. When a candidate visits the site, besides the mine of information available, the candidate can click on the online store button or paste the following in their browser www.ncbex2.org/catalog.

The candidate will find sample MBEs offered for sale.

It's a good idea to purchase some or all the MBE's on the site. There are not very many but there are also samples of essays and especially performance tests to buy. These have very useful analyses of the correct answers.

Even more past essay and performance test questions can be used free of charge at www.calbar.ca.gov. Two passing answers are published for each question. We wrote 6 of those model essays for one bar exam. Plus two model performance tests.

The MBEs offered for purchase on www.ncbex.org are particularly important both to all candidates since most bars do not publish past MBE questions as they're usually copyrighted.

With regard to answering and re-answering the same available MBEs, because the candidate will see the correct answers several times during the many attempts, after four or five go-arounds the candidate should start striving to get all the answers correct.
When the candidate begins to get 85 to 100%

of the answers correct after such repetition, the candidate's confidence will be up and just as important, the candidate will have developed a comfortable familiarity with examination-level MBEs.

In this material an analysis of each question is presented after the choices, among other purposes to ignite the candidate's thought process or point out pit falls that must be avoided in reasoning.

Finally, states differ on what substantive law is tested on the MBE. Some states include state law while others don't.

For example on the California MBE the FRE is assumed, the UCC applies, comparative negligence with joint and several liability applies, and the Federal constitution is in force.

.

Answer key

1. B 2. A 3. B 4. A 5. C 6. C 7. B 8. B 9. D 10. A
11. C 12. A 13. D 14. C 15. C 16. C 17. B 18. B 19. C
Value bar bonus question A
20. A
21. C 22. C 23. B 24. D 25. D 26. A 27. D 28. D 29. D
30. B
31. C 32. A 33. B 34. A 35. A 36. A 37. B 38. C 39. D 40.
A
41. A 42. B 43. C 44. A 45. A 46. D 47. A 48. C. 49. B 50.
D
51. D 52. A 53. C 54. D 55. D 56. C 57. D 58. A 59. A 60.
C
61. D 62. C 63. B 64. A 65. A 66. D 67. B 68. D 69. A 70.
B
71. A 72. C 73. A 74. B 75. A 76. A 77. C 78. C 79. A 80.
C
81. B 82. B 83. A 84. B 85. C 86. B 87. A 88. B 89. A 90.
D
91. C 92. C 93. A 94. A 95. A 96. A 97. D 98. D 99. A 99.
D 100. A
Bonus Question. C Bonus Question. B

1. During winter Pete asked Den whom he knew to be a careful driver to drive Pete to hospital in Pete's car. Den agreed. At an intersection where a 5-car pile-up recently occurred and in which Pete's sister Madge died, Den drove Pete's car into the side of a furniture truck.

In a negligence action brought by Pete against Den, Pete loses because

(A) Pete did not assume a risk of injury
(B) Pete suffered no physical injury
(C) Den drove Pete's car carefully on previous occasions with Pete in it
(D) Den can be sued under both negligence and negligence per se

Analysis

The red herrings here are easy to spot. Note that on the bar the first few questions are often straightforward with clearly avoidable wrong answers.

There is ordinarily no negligence liability if there is no bodily injury or property damage regardless of previous safety or danger, regardless of plaintiff's possible claims, or an assumption of risk, or proof of duty, breach or causation.

2. City has enacted a zoning ordinance which prohibits gambling within half a mile of any school, church or bar.
The ordinance was signed by the mayor last week. Before the passage of the ordinance Fred legally operated a small casino adjacent to his restaurant. Fred's restaurant has a bar that serves only non alcoholic drinks. The casino is now illegal.
Fred's challenge to the ordinance will succeed because

(A) The ordinance provides no amortization period
(B) The ordinance is a total but compensated taking of Fred's property
(C) The ordinance provides an unreasonably lengthy
amortization period
(D) The ordinance is facially invalid as applied

Analysis

No time to recoup loses occasioned by new zoning will help the property owner.

3. City has enacted a zoning ordinance which prohibits gambling within half a mile of any school, church or bar. The ordinance was signed by the mayor last week.
Before the passage of the ordinance Fred legally operated a small casino adjacent to his restaurant. Fred's restaurant has a bar that serves only non alcoholic drinks. The casino is now illegal.
Fred's challenge to the ordinance will fail because

(A) Fred's business is protected under the dormant commerce clause
(B) The ordinance is rationally related to a legitimate government purpose
(C) The ordinance places an undue burden on the rights of city church members to practice their religion
(D) Non alcoholic drinks are exempted under the ordinance

Analysis

Under a state's general police power, zoning regulations are usually analyzed under the rationality standard.

4. A man went into a store and ordered a cigar. He paid for the cigar. The man went out of the store and got in his car.
He drove into the street. The man then realized that he did not collect his cigar. He went back to the store but did not obtain it. The man has now sued the store for conversion of his cigar. Will he succeed?

(A) Yes because the man paid for the cigar and has futilely demanded it
(B) Yes because the store clerk gave the man the cigar when the man paid for it
(C) Yes because the man collected the cigar
(D) Yes because the store clerk asserts that the man collected the cigar

Analysis

Conversion consists of an act constituting a substantial interference with or deprivation of, plaintiff's property so serious that the tort feasor must pay the entire value.
Ownership of purchased personal property ordinarily passes with the payment of the purchase price even without physical delivery.

Thus the rights of the new owner can be violated even by the seller of the item because he has transferred ownership.

5. A federal law gives authority to states to allow an undocumented alien to purchase a marriage license only if the undocumented alien first pays a fine for being in the country without documented authorization. Is this law constitutional?

(A) No. A federal law must pass judicial scrutiny before it may bind a state
(B) No. Under the supremacy clause a state's law may preempt federal law on the issuance of state marriage licenses
(C) No. A federal law cannot commandeer a state to enforce federal fines
(D) No. A state has no power to deny a guaranteed right as applied to citizens of the United States

Analysis

Because of the federal character of the constitution the federal government cannot commandeer a state's power to do federal functions.

Note that no judicial analysis of an act of congress is required before the act goes into effect - unless of course the act itself provides otherwise.

6. Acme Inc is a registered charity in the state. Dan contracted with Acme Inc to supply 20 pounds of cough vaccine to all fourteen dormitories of State University on March 7. On March 8 Charles, a State University student living in a dormitory, suffered a cough-induced seizure and died in his sleep. On March 11 Dan delivered 20 pounds of safe cough vaccine to all fourteen dormitories of State University. In a dispute between the estate of Charles and Dan the best ground for a tort action is

(A) Strict product liability
(B) Negligent infliction of emotional distress
(C) Negligence arising from breach of a contract duty
(D) Medical battery

Analysis

A negligence action succeeds if there is physical harm or property damage foreseeably or directly caused by failure to exercise proper reasonable care, special or ordinary, in a setting requiring due care.

The issues here include whether the plaintiff's injury was foreseeable to one in Dan's position as well as whether Dan's actions are even a cause in fact of the harm suffered. In answering, consider if Charles was an intended beneficiary of the breached delivery contract.

7. The action by the estate of Charles in question 6 will succeed if

(A) The estate proves that Den wrongfully breached its contract with ACME and that Charles was an intended beneficiary

(B) The estate proves that Den wrongfully breached its
duty to ACME and this proximately caused foreseeable
injury to Charles

(C) The estate proves that Acme wrongly breached its contract with ACME without justifiable excuse amounting to conversion of the vaccines

(D) ACME proves that it rightfully paid Ben for the vaccines

Analysis

The standard of care for ordinary negligence is the reasonable person standard. A gross deviation from this standard may be ruled reckless.

8. Ariel, aged 34, contacts Barry, aged 31. Ariel tells Barry that he intends to rob a store in the next town with Barry's help. Barry has known Ariel for over seventeen years and does not believe that Ariel would rob a store. Barry is an expert locksmith and owns a gun. Barry's gun is highly accurate when fired from close range. Which of the following statements is NOT true?

(A) Barry is not Ariel's accomplice
(B) Barry is Ariel's accomplice
(C) Ariel has committed a crime
(D) Barry has not committed a crime

Analysis

When both a state of mind must be present and an actual criminal act must occur for a crime to be committed, that crime is committed only when the necessary state of mind induces a criminal act. In a robbery context an act is required but did Ariel do such an act? Did Barry? Even applying the accomplice rules to the candidate's answer, what is the conclusion?

The candidate should be familiar with the rules on the crime of solicitation to understand why (C) is true and thus not the correct response.

9.Watcher agreed to 'watch' Dot, a 7 yearold, while Dot's wealthy mother, Mom, went across the road to post a letter in the mail box on that side of the road. Before Mom reached the mail box she heard Dot give a shout. Mom spun round in time to see Watcher fall into the path of a speeding cyclist.
The cyclist's best claim against Mom is

(A) Negligent entrustment of Dot to another person
(B) Duress excusing bodily harm to the cyclist
(C) Negligent breach of a duty owed to both Watcher and Dot
(D) Negligent breach of a foreseeable duty owed to the cyclist

Analysis

Foreseeability is vital in Negligence whether duty is found under the Andrew's duty to the whole world, or under Cardozo's zone of danger rule.

10. On Tuesday last week Andrew was stopped by a police officer on suspicion of walking in a no-pedestrian section of a road. The police officer warned Andrew of the danger that Andrew was exposing himself and other road-users to.
As the police officer turned back to the patrol car he caught sight of something that might have been a knife gleaming in Andrew's shirt pocket. The police officer asked Andrew if he was carrying a knife. Andrew replied that he would not answer.

Is the police officer permitted to continue questioning Andrew?

(A) Yes, based on reasonable suspicion derived from a plain view
(B) Yes but only if Andrew can be said to be in custody at that moment
(C) Yes but only if Andrew reasonably believed that he was not free to go

(D) Yes but only based on the police officer's knowledge of articulable facts requiring a search of Andrew's person

Analysis

Where an officer is standing in a public place where he has a right to be anything he sees in his natural line of sight without extraordinary means is in plain view. A Miranda issue arises only if there is custody such as a formal arrest or a mandatory detention. A sixth amendment problem arises only at critical stages after judicial proceedings have started.

11. Pete was hit and injured by a car driven by Derek at an intersection in the city center. The defendant Derek has counterclaimed against the plaintiff Pete.
In defending against Derek's counterclaim can Pete introduce Winnie's statement that Winnie is the Derek's accountant to help prove the Derek's income?

(A) No because Derek's claim is a counter claim
(B) No because the statement does not prove

Pete's income
(C) Yes even though the statement does not prove Pete's income by itself
(D) No even though Winnie has personal knowledge

Analysis

Under the FRE (and on the California bar presently) evidence is admissible if it has any tendency to make a disputed fact more or less probable than without it. If Pete's income is in issue, Winnie's employment as Pete's accountant is logically relevant to any evidence about Pete's income. It will also relevant to challenging any testimony on the point. Moreover evidence of her employment makes her testimony credible.

12. A taxi cab driver was robbed at gun point on Tuesday.
On Saturday the police showed the taxi cab driver a photograph of a female and asked him if he recognized the person in the picture. When the taxi cab driver answered yes the police asked him who the person in the picture was. The taxi cab driver answered that the person in the photograph was his wife. If the cab driver's wife is

arrested the cab driver would lose
his home to foreclosure. On Monday the taxi
cab driver and his wife left the
jurisdiction permanently.

Is the taxi cab driver's identification
admissible in the later prosecution of a
defendant for the robbery of
another cab?

(A) Yes as a statement against interest
(B) No because there was probable cause for
the driver's interrogation
(C) No because the identification was made
without Miranda warnings and the taxi cab
driver was not in custody
(D) No because the taxi cab driver did not
have his lawyer present nor was his wife's
lawyer present

Analysis

A statement is against interest if hurts either
the penal interest or the penal interest of its
maker. In California social disgrace is
included. Here the cabbie is unavailable,
the statement is claimed to be against his
pecuniary interests. As to (D), Sixth

amendment issues do not arise here because no judicial proceedings ever started against the cab driver. (B) does not address the issue raised.

13. A man made a gift of real property to his two nephews as joint tenants with right of survivorship. The two nephews moved onto the property immediately but after several years they disagreed about the apportionment of property taxes. One of the nephews brought an action for a declaration that both owners owed all taxes equally. The court granted the declaration requested. What is now the state of title to the property?

(A) The nephews are now tenants in common with right of survivorship
(B) The nephews are now tenants in common without right of survivorship
(C) The nephews are common law joint tenants but the property is held without right of survivorship
(D) The nephews are joint tenants and the property is held with right of survivorship

Analysis

A joint tenancy features a right of

survivorship that can be
broken by conveyance of a share to a non
joint-tenant, by
agreement or by operation of law. The key is
that there is
an intent to end the joint tenancy and splinter
the shares
into individual portions.

14. Principal sent a fax to Agent requesting
Agent to obtain certain global positioning
equipment from a local volume
seller, instal it for Principal's customer by a
certain date, and then bill Principal on the
customary terms prevailing between the
Principal and the agent.
In a subsequent action between Principal and
Agent if the issue is the existence of a valid
agency contract, the UCC

(A) Governs because the Agent will argue
that he performed his part of the agreement
while the Principal without excuse did not
perform his part
(B) Applies only to the Principal's
performance on these facts
(C) Does not apply to either the Principal or
the Agent as to whether they formed an

agency contract between themselves
(D) Applies only to the agent's performance
on these facts

Analysis

On these facts the UCC would apply only if
there was a sale of goods. The UCC also
governs some security interests but the facts
here are clear.
15. At 10 : 30 p.m. a night club worker
planted an explosive under a patron's car and
set it to go off in three hours. At midnight it
began to rain. The rain rendered the
explosives ineffective and they did not work.
At the trial of the night club worker she can
be convicted of

(A) Criminal battery
(B) Criminal assault
(C) Attempted criminal battery
(D) Attempted criminal acts

Analysis

An attempt is characterized by 1) the intent to
commit the target crime 2) the failure of a
substantial step then taken.
A criminal battery is an intentional or reckless

infliction of a harmful or offensive contact - without excuse of justification. Legal excuses and justifications include self defense, defense of others and prevention of crime. What might be a legal justification or excuse under these facts?

16. At 05 : 35 a.m. a disgruntled distribution company employee planted an explosive under his estranged fiancee's trailer, timing it to go off in two days to give him time to travel to another state and hide. It soon began to snow. The falling snow rendered the explosives ineffective and they did not go off. At the trial of the employee the least serious homicide offense he can be convicted of is

(A) Felony Murder
(B) Involuntary manslaughter
(C) Attempted murder
(D) Premeditated criminal battery

Analysis

You should quickly see that on the facts there is no completed crime. For instance there is no battery since there was no contact with anybody's person. Involuntary manslaughter is an unintended killing

resulting from negligence, the commission of
a misdemeanor or an unlawful act like nondeadly
battery. It is less serious than murder
or attempted murder - but here no
one died.

17. A lawyer took a client to dinner to discuss
the client's planned sale of stocks. The client
told the lawyer that if the lawyer could
structure the sale to avoid certain state taxes,
the client would increase the lawyer's
compensation by 13%. With respect to the
compensation previously agreed
between the lawyer and the client the client's
present statement is

(A) An offer to revoke the previous
compensation agreement
(B) An offer to modify the previous
compensation agreement
(C) An offer to settle the dispute regarding the
previous compensation agreement and thus
the offer of an accord and satisfaction
(D) A promise not showing enough
commitment to qualify as an offer

Analysis

On the facts the client's statement does not

intend to revoke any previous agreement, nor is there a dispute reported in the facts.

Unlike the UCC under common law - which controls a non sale of goods situation like this - a modification is ineffective without new consideration. The desired stock sale structuring here would constitute such consideration.

Note that these days the absence of consideration would not by itself remove the right to make an offer because the contract can be ruled void for lack of consideration if consideration is not later agreed.

18. A landowner entered into a signed agreement permitting the owner of an adjoining parcel of land to build a child's bird cage on the landowner's property at any time during the next 6 months subject to the payment of $400. The bird cage would be removed after one year. This agreement may be found to be

(A) A periodic tenancy unenforceable because of the statute of frauds
(B) A license, an easement appurtenant or an

easement in gross
(C) An easement created by adverse
possession
(D) An equitable servitude restricting both
parcels of land to residential use only

Analysis

A periodic tenancy runs from period to period
automatically. Here there is only a single oneyear
term.
There has been no hostile, open, actual, or
continuos possession for any length of time
and so no AP.
Equitable servitudes require an agreement
limiting land use made as landowners with
lateral privity, intent, notice and writing -
and do not apply here.

A license is an unenforceable permission to
use another's land (there are exceptions to
enforceability such as expenditure via
detrimental reliance), and an easement is
an enforceable agreement to use another's
land for ease of access to the dominant parcel.
A circumstance could be a license or an
easement but not both at the same time.

19. A warehouse worker entered a restricted

part of the warehouse to smoke a cigarette in a restricted area hidden from view of the rest of the warehouse. The warehouse worker did not want to be seen by anyone because he was not yet on his break. A few minutes after the warehouse worker went back to his work a fire started in one of the warehouse bathrooms. At the warehouse worker's trial which of the following evidence is admissible?

(A) A firefighter's report written after thoroughly investigating the fire
(B) The fire marshal's report written after thoroughly investigating the fire
(C) The fire department's entry of responding to the fire in its own daily records
(C) The warehouse worker's scientific opinion as to the technical causes of warehouse bathroom fires

Analysis

The fruits of a government investigation or a government agent's official observations cannot be used against a criminal defendant under the FRE (under CA's CEC they can.) But a government agency's record of its own activities can be so used.

Note that it's unlikely for an ordinary warehouse worker to be accepted as an expert witness concerning technical causes of warehouse bathroom fires because fires are not his area of knowledge, skill, experience, training, or education. FRE 702.

Value bar bonus question:

A policeman took a cruise on a large ship with thousands of other holiday makers. The police man went into a bathroom to inject a legal body-building steroid into his arm. When he finished, he threw the used syringe down the toilet and flushed it. A few minutes later a fire broke out in that bathroom. Two holiday makers died from the effects of the fire as it spread through the ship.
At the policeman's trial which of the following evidence is admissible to prove arson?

(A) A statement by a witness tending to show that the policeman acted maliciously
(B) A statement by a witness tending to show that the policeman did not act maliciously or with indifference to the value of life
(C) A statement by a person with personal

knowledge tending to show that the
policeman acted without indifference to the
value of human life
(D) A statement by a witness corroborated by
the fact that the fire actually occurred

Analysis

At common law arson is the malicious
burning of another person's dwelling. Malice
means wrongful, illegal,
reckless etc - not moral wickedness, spite or
hate.
Often, a cruise ship would be another
person's dwelling for arson purposes because
other people besides the defendant sleep on it.

20. A mother who died testate devised her
land in fee simple to her four daughters as
tenants in common and provided that if any
one of the tenants ever sold or gave
away her share to anyone including the other
tenants, that tenant would forfeit her share
and it would go to the remaining tenants or if
none to the mothers'
nephew, a man named Neff, or to Neff's
surviving children.
Can the forfeiture provision be severed from
the grant?

(A) Yes if the court deems it a complete restraint on alienation

(A) Yes if the court does not deem it a complete restraint on alienation

(C) Yes if the court finds that it does not violate the rule against perpetuities

(D) Yes if the court finds that the rule of Worthier Title applies so that the mother has the fee simple reversion

Analysis

Courts generally frown on conditions attached to a conveyance if those conditions mean that the land is no longer available for commerce, new ownership or for whatever the courts deem it important for land to be available for in the area. See Havard Law Review Vol. XLVIII January 1935 No. 3.

21. A jurisdiction's statute provides as follows: "The maker of a will must sign it in the presence of two witnesses who, being both present at the same time, know that the testator is signing his will and who receive no gift or other interest under the will." A testator in the jurisdiction signed a will in the presence of one witness. The

testator then died.

When the will was offered for probate, the probate clerk correctly stated that while the fee for probating a will with two witnesses was $50, the fee for probating a will with one witness was $90. The testator's personal representative has chosen to file a constitutional challenge.

The court inquires into whether the difference in fees violates the constitution.

The correct level of scrutiny is

(A) Strict scrutiny since access to probate court is fundamental in that state

(B) Mid-level review since access to probate court is within the quasi-suspect class of classification

(C) Rationality because no suspect class, quasi-suspect class or fundamental right is involved

(D) No scrutiny is required because the inequality in fees is facially invalid

Analysis

Access to certain courts is a fundamental right. Examples are divorce court and criminal court.

The suspect classes are race, alienage in some

cases, and national origin. Fundamental rights include the first amendment, the penumbra of privacy, the right to migrate interstate, access to criminal justice and divorce courts, the right to vote.

Art IV P&I rights include the rights fundamental to national unity such as the right to work, practice a profession or do business in any state. Rights that are not fundamental are usually scrutinized at the rational basis level but a few have been scrutinized at something akin to mid level review.

For instance in Rosario v. Rockefeller 410 US 752 (1973) by a 5-4 decision the Supreme court reversed the district court by upholding a voter law which it said served an 'important' - not rational - goal of New York state.
Answer (D) sounds logical and reasonable but represents no known legal doctrine.

On the facts only a fee dispute exists - not any of the fundamental rights mentioned above.

22. A plaintiff filed a motion challenging the

propriety of the defendant's discovery request. The request was for the production of medical bills incurred on account of injuries sustained when plaintiff fell off an improvised cardboard ladder while repairing a high book case. The medical bills were very low in amount.

Will the plaintiff recover from the book case manufacturer in strict product liability for failure to warn of injury?

(A) No because the medical bills were low
(B) Yes because the medical bills were low, showing that the plaintiff's injuries were not serious
(C) No because a warning by the manufacturer of the book case would not have added anything to the obvious dangers of an improvised cardboard ladder
(D) No because the medical bills must be authenticated to be admissible in evidence

Analysis

Although all written evidence must be authenticated just as oral evidence must have a proper foundation, neither of these issues is relevant here. A proper warning is not a defense to defective design or manufacture, but if it would help prevent injury or reduce danger, it's a defect not to have it. Nevertheless if a warning would not have any safety-enhancing effect - as where the danger of injury is obvious - its absence will not be a defect.

23. A fruit seller agreed to sell and a fruit buyer agreed to buy 10 pounds of fruit, to be delivered to the buyer's home in time for the buyer's graduation party. The fruit seller was unable to obtain the fruit she envisaged and promptly informed the fruit buyer, who soon forgot all about what the fruit seller told her. The fruit buyer was disappointed when there was no fruit at her graduation party and called the fruit seller, who offered to deliver the next day. If the fruit buyer prevails in an action for damages it will be because

(A) The fruit seller offered to deliver the fruit on the day of the graduation party
(B) The fruit seller's inability to obtain the fruit she envisaged did not excuse her nonperformance
(C) The fruit buyer forgot all about what the fruit seller told her concerning the fruit seller's inability to obtain the fruit she

envisaged
(D) The fruit buyer paid for delivery of the 10 pounds of fruit in advance

Analysis

Answer (A) mocks the facts. Answer (C) is factually accurate but contains nothing that answers the interrogatory. Answer (D) is not shown by the facts.

24. A man inherited land with a hotel on it in fee simple absolute.
Another man owned adjacent land with a store on it. The first man allowed the second man to cross the first man's land to reach a private road because they both
belonged to a club situated on that road. The second man sold his land to a third man. The relevant deed from the
second man to the third man incorrectly stated that the land being conveyed benefitted from an easement over the first
man's land and that the first man's land was in danger of subsidence.
If the first man wins an action against the second man for publishing the statement about subsidence it will be because

(A) The land being conveyed benefitted only
from a license
(B) The second man was negligent in giving
an incorrect deed
(C) The first man's hotel was disparaged by
the statement in the deed given by the second
man
(D) The first man lost customers and profits
as a result of the statement in the deed

Analysis

Note that only the interrogatory and the
answer choices identify the question as a tort question - the
facts do not.
Look out for this sort of question. Trade libel
is not often tested but be prepared.
(A) and (B) are accurate but do not explain
why the plaintiff wins for a false statement
about subsidence on his business land.
(C) is a good answer but disparagement of
goods and business by false statement will
not be compensated at common law without
proof of actual business losses.

25. A law of the jurisdiction states in part:
"An unrecorded conveyance or other grant is
void against a subsequent purchaser in good
faith who provides valuable consideration and

whose interest is recorded first." Anne
bought land from a government agency. Anne
properly recorded the deed.
The agency sold the same land to Beth who
recorded.
Beth, the second purchaser, brought a timely
action against Anne to quiet title. The court
improperly determined that although Anne
bought and recorded before the Beth,
Beth's subsequent interest had priority. The
court action cost Anne $40,000.
Anne has sued Beth for malicious institution
of civil proceedings.
Who wins?

(A) Beth because the court determined that
her interest had priority
(B) Beth because she sued Beth to establish
ownership of the land
(C) Beth because her suit did not unduly
harass or harm Anne
(D) Beth because she has proved all the
statements above

Analysis

The facts here are deliberately dense - but the
choices are straight forward. Look out for
such on the examination.

The action did not end in Anne's favor. On that basis alone she ordinarily would not win a suit for malicious prosecution notwithstanding that her failure to win was because of a wrong decision by the court.

26. Dotty suffered a broken arm when Adam, who was carrying a baby up a flight of stairs to escape a snow storm, stumbled into 76 year-old Dotty. Dotty brought a tort action against Adam which was dismissed. The City attorney then brought a misdemeanor charge of making a false police report against Dotty. If Dotty makes a confession of a previous manslaughter during the misdemeanor false report trial the confession will be

(A) Excluded as not relevant
(B) Authenticated by appropriate evidence in order to be admissible
(C) Admitted as relevant and not misleading to the jury
(D) Admitted as reputation evidence of Dotty's past character

Analysis

Evidence must be relevant, non prejudicial, not capable of causing delay, confusion of issues or misleading of the jury, to be admitted. What would be the relevance of a previous manslaughter in a trial for making a false police report based on different facts? This is a relevance issue.

All other complications can safely be ignored.

27. The defendant has offered evidence that at the time of the robbery he was sixty miles from the town where a gas station was robbed. The state has objected to admitting the evidence on the ground that the defendant previously told detectives he was in another place only twenty miles away. This is the first the jury has been told of this conflict.

When the defendant spoke to detectives he was in a police cell and in leg shackles. The court should

(A) Sustain the objection on grounds of prior inconsistent testimony since the two alibis conflict and this is perjury

(B) Admit the evidence because it pertains to the state's defense. No inconsistent testimony is before the court

(C) Sustain the objection because it was timely made and an offer of proof is implied - the jury can prove the evidence offered

(D) Admit the evidence because the defendant is proffering it in his defense and the state's objection relies on statements not in evidence

Analysis

Under the FRE, Prior Inconsistent Testimony ('PIS') can be used to impeach no matter how made, but is substantively admitted for its truth only if made under oath
at a previous trial, hearing or deposition.
A jury never proves anything nor ever makes any offer to prove anything. Only lawyers for parties 'offer proof of evidence' when the judge sustains an objection. Note that
 if an objection is overruled, the lawyer making it no longer has to 'take an exception' in order to challenge the ruling on appeal.

In a criminal trial the state never presents a defense but only prosecutes.
Consider: If a fact is not in evidence in a criminal trial, will the court prejudice a defendant by disallowing his vital

alibi evidence based on a conflict allegedly known to the prosecution? Or will the court rather invite the prosecution
to impeach the defendant's story with whatever other story it knows?

On a CA essay question the candidate must bear prop 8 in mind and comment on it.

28 A criminal defendant presents evidence that he was stopped as he drove away from a car wash by a plain clothes police officer. The officer told the defendant that he was being arrested for a serious battery on a man two days earlier. The officer
ordered the defendant out of the his car. While the defendant stood beside the car, the officer searched the entire front of the defendant's car. He found a bloody bicycle chain under the driver's seat. The defendant moves to suppress the bicycle chain. The court

(A) Will suppress because the search was incident to arrest
(B) Will suppress because the officer was entitled to search for contraband
(C) Will suppress because the defendant was not in handcuffs and could have reached a

weapon inside the car

(D) Will not suppress because the defendant was not in handcuffs and could have reached a weapon inside the car

Analysis

(A) and (B) and (C) are legally illogical - the facts and legal conclusions are at odds. However, when a driver is arrested but is not handcuffed he could still reach a weapon inside the car. Because of this the police are entitled to search for a weapon in the driver's area and the passenger compartment (which will probably logically not exclude under the driver's seat).

Even if under the driver's seat is not to be logically included in these areas, the police will respond that items there are in plain view at least from the passenger's compartment. Moreover, if the police have probable cause to suspect weapons like a gun (not immediately apparent on these facts as defendant was only coming out of a car wash) they will argue that they have a right to search under the driver's seat where it is very likely to be stashed.

The police are almost never allowed to search for general evidence of crime except with probable cause or during a stop such as this on proper suspicion that the car has in it evidence of the crime for which the stop was made in the first place.

However only places and things capable of containing the items sought can be searched. Thus ordinarily, there will be no searching of the glove compartment looking for a stolen 40-inch screen television.

29. Newspaper columnist and Neighbor agreed that Neighbor would not contract for the delivery to the neighbor's home of any magazines or newspapers without telling Newspaper columnist.
Newspaper columnist wanted this agreement because she distributed the newspaper she worked for. Newspaper columnist made the same agreement with all the other neighbors.

Is this a restrictive covenant affecting the use of the parties' neighboring properties?

(A) Yes because each property owner is

forbidden to do something she would
otherwise have a right to do
(B) Yes because each property owner has
notice and an intent to bind future owners
(C) No because a restrictive covenant must be
properly recorded to be valid
(D) No

Analysis

A restrictive covenant affecting the use of
property must touch and concern actual use of
the land. Ordinarily, newspaper deliveries are
not an aspect of use of land as an
agreement not to build a parking lot or to
demolish one would be.

30. Two women agreed to rob a night club as
soon as it opened.
The two women carried out the robbery and
hid in a nearby alley for several hours until
the police departed.
The two women then stole a car and drove to
another state where they stayed at a hotel
until they had spent all the proceeds of the
robbery on clothes and jewelry. Two years
later the two women were charged with
conspiracy and robbery.
What result?

(A) They can be convicted of either conspiracy or robbery but not both

(B) They can be convicted of both conspiracy and robbery

(C) They can be convicted of robbery

(D) They can be convicted of conspiracy

Analysis

Conspiracy is a stand-alone offense that doesn't merge into any subsequent crime.

31. A 4 year-old boy and her mother were visiting the boy's uncle at an army base. His uncle was an amateur clown and entertained the boy while his concerned mother watched. The boy's uncle accidentally poked the boy's mother in the eye while performing a routine. The boy can sue for

(A) His emotional distress

(B) His physical injuries

(C) His emotional distress because he was in the zone of danger

(D) His economic losses

Analysis

A person can recover for their own emotional distress at seeing a family member injured or threatened with injury if they were themselves in the zone of danger and/or the actor knew that the plaintiff was present. These are not the only situations in which this statutory tort can be committed. See California Jury Instructions 1620.

32. A city enacted an ordinance requiring new welfare payees to have lived in either the city or the state for at least one week with an intent to remain in either the state or the city for the foreseeable future. The restriction applies only to payees seeking city housing assistance.
A long time resident of the city who wants new City housing assistance has challenged the ordinance on equal protection grounds.

(A) The long time resident has no standing unless he intends to live outside the city or the state in the foreseeable future
(B) The long time resident has standing because he is certain to suffer an injury in fact under the new ordinance
(C) The dispute is not yet ripe for adjudication
(D) The dispute is ripe for adjudication
Analysis
Choice (B) is conclusory without facts.

For standing there must be harm or at least a concrete chance of individuated harm, redressable-ness, and a claim that the defendant did the wrong.

33. President of Convention Supplies sent a reply fax to General Manager of Computer Works. The reply fax said in pertinent part: "The installation was acceptable but ran over the contract stipulated time by over three hours. That cost us thirty-six hundred dollars because of all our conventioneers who could not connect to the internet. It would be reasonable for you to reimburse us."

On receiving this fax, General Manager immediately contacted President by telephone. The parties reached an agreement to submit the matter to arbitration. If Convention Supply Co brings an action against Computer Works Inc before the arbitration date for breach of contract which of the following is true?

(A) Convention Supply Co will lose because at common law a modification requires consideration to be effective
(B) Computer Works Inc will lose because the

installation was not timely

(C) Neither party is bound by the results of the arbitration

(D) The arbitration term is material and thus never became part of the contract

Analysis

Since the parties have a dispute, the arbitration agreement can be seen as an accord. If so, Convention Supply Co can perform the accord (go to arbitration) or refuse and sue on the original claim.
The arbitration agreement has no impact on whether the contract was breached.

34. Kitchens is a well known caterer in City. Hotel Presidential is on the same commercial street as Kitchens.
In March, Kitchens agreed with Hotel Presidential to share the costs of video surveillance of the street equally. The arrangement worked satisfactorily for 2 years. In July Kitchens informed Hotel Presidential that it would no longer participate in the arrangement since police patrols of the area were now adequate to deter crime. Hotel Presidential demanded that Kitchens

submit to arbitration.

Because Hotel Presidential was also a valued customer, Kitchens agreed. The arbitrator concluded that

1) The police patrols were inadequate
2) The video surveillance agreement was enforceable and
3) The video surveillance agreement was not within the statute of frauds because:

(A) It could have been completely performed in one day
(B) It could have been completely performed in over one year
(C) It was not an unconscionable agreement
(D) It was not intended to modify any preexisting agreement

Analysis

That a contract is or is not conscionable has no effect on whether it must be evidenced by a writing under the statute of frauds. That an agreement modifies or does not modify an earlier contract similarly has no SOF effect.

Apart from the one year rule other contracts

caught by the SOF are contracts in which marriage is consideration, land contracts actually transferring interests, executors' contracts and agreements by a guarantor to pay the debt of another where the guarantor's main purpose is not to benefit himself.

35. Motor cycle dealer was about to go out of business and decided to sell his motor home and move. Motor cycle dealer advertised for a buyer in the local papers intending to sell it himself, without the help of professional agents.
Motor cycle dealer's advertisements declared that he would not consider selling to any buyer of Latin origin.
What constitutional issues are raised under the thirteenth amendment?

(A) Whether the sale of a motor home is a badge and incident of slavery
(B) No issues are raised under the thirteenth amendment
(C) Whether congress has acted under the necessary and proper clause
(D) The facts are subject to strict scrutiny review based on race, a suspect class

Analysis

The badges and incidents of slavery are determined by congress and are vitally relevant to 13th amendment analysis. The facts here do not include any actions by a government.
While the 13th amendment can uniquely reach non-state private action such as the behavior of a motor home seller but only if an incident or badge of slavery is involved.

36. In a class-certification hearing related to a mass tort suit, Professor D. Lorne states on direct examination that the book Standard Theories of Tort Law is an authority he has professionally relied on for 20 years. He quotes the book in his testimony. This means that

(A) Standard Theories of Tort Law can be read into evidence under the federal rules of evidence
(B) Standard Theories of Tort Law is an out of court statement admissible only under present sense impression if Lorne reads it to the jury before he has been dismissed from giving evidence in the case

(C) Standard Theories of Tort Law is subject to the rule of Crawford v Washington. It can not be admitted unless Lorne is available for cross examination now or was available at the time he read Standard Theories of Tort Law
(D) Standard Theories of Contract Law has been overruled by the supreme court case of Pennoyer v Neff

Analysis

You must be aware that a statement expressing a present sense impression is always made out of court, never in court, and is a 'statement describing or explaining an event or condition made while the declarant was perceiving the event or condition, or immediately thereafter.' FRE 803.
Crawford v Washington relates to the admissibility of certain testimonial statements not challenged by an accused at trial or at the time of their making under criminal procedure.
Pennoyer v Neff is irrelevant here. It decided that a court may enter a judgment against a non-resident of a state if the party is personally served with process while within the state, or property he has within the state is

brought under the court's jurisdiction before
the action starts.

37. A and B own adjoining properties on a
lake front.
There is a disused landfill nearby. A's
children agree with B's children to play
within the sections of the landfill
where it is convenient to play. All the children
then begin playing in the landfill. it has no
security or other guards. If
the agreement between the children is
claimed to be a covenant between A and B
which of the following is true?

(A) The 'covenant' touches and concerns
their properties because the two properties are
in close proximity
(B) The 'covenant' does not touch and
concern their properties because no duty has
been accepted by either party which would
affect use of their own land
(C) The 'covenant' is enforceable although
oral
(D) The 'covenant' is unenforceable because
it has been partly performed

Under property law a land covenant must
have two principals who are in privity such as
seller and buyer, landlord and tenant, the
agreement must affect how the land is used or
treated.
If it affects the value of the land this can be
enough. If there is any question of a
subsequent occupier being bound, an intent to
bind such a person must be shown. The
covenant must be written.

With equitable servitudes and restrictive
equitable easements no initial horizontal
privity is required so that a
later occupier can inherit the duties or
benefits of a former one based only on notice
- but vertical privity between the
first occupier and the later occupier must
exist, plus notice and intent to bind that
second occupier.

The real difference between an equitable
agreement -
which is effective against a later occupier
through notice, and a land covenant -
which is effective against a latter occupier if
he is stated to be bound - whether he has
notice or not - is that breach of a land
covenant means money damages whereas an

equitable servitude or restriction can be specifically enforced.

38. A and B own adjoining properties on a lake front.
There is a disused landfill nearby. A's children agree with B's children to play within the sections of the landfill where it is convenient to play. All the children begin playing in the landfill. It has no security or other guards.
If Bob, one of B's children, falls into a shallow ravine while playing in the landfill and sues A, the likely result is that:

(A) Bob will be found to be an intended beneficiary of the covenant between A and B
(B) Bob will win against A for maintaining an attractive nuisance.
(C) Bob's suit will be dismissed because the landfill is not maintained by A.
(D) Even if there is a covenant between A and B, Bob will sue both on the basis of maintaining an attractive nuisance.

Analysis

There are no "intended beneficiaries" under land covenants, only "heirs, future assigns".

As a technical matter, a contract and a
covenant are not the same thing.
Among other elements, liability for an
attractive nuisance arises where a landowner
knows that children are likely to
be trespassing or are already doing so.

39. When a United States citizen is arrested
for several suspected crimes, that citizen can
not be questioned for which of those crimes
until Miranda warnings have been
given?

(A) Crimes for which he has not been
arrested
(B) Crimes for which he is in custody
(C) Crimes which he did not commit as
principal
(D) Any of the crimes

Analysis

The requirement to give Miranda warnings
kicks in from the moment of custody. It is a
bright line rule (mandatory.)
Therefore if there is custody and questioning
occurs without the required warnings the rule
is broken. This would be the case whatever
crime is asked about because the same rights

are implicated whatever the crime.
However if the defendant knowingly and
intelligently waives his rights he can be
questioned about any crime at
all whether he was expecting to be questioned
about that particular crime or not. He cannot
assert his rights piecemeal offense-by-offense
like a child choosing a favorite toy.
Note that un-Mirandized statements can still
be used to impeach, while physical and livewitness
fruit of an unwarned confession (but
not of a search) will often be admitted even if
the confession itself is thrown out. A
confession may be thrown out for being
coerced or unwarned.

40. It is not necessary for an injured plaintiff
to show which of two ice hockey opponents
inflicted his serious injury if:

(A) The injured plaintiff did not see how he
got injured at the time of the game
(B) The plaintiff negligently did not ask who
injured him but the defendants have
stipulated that the plaintiff could
not have seen the contact
(C) The injured plaintiff recklessly failed to
realize which team mate injured him
(D) The court determines that the plaintiff

was also harmfully negligent

Analysis

You should consider that the plaintiff's failure to ask which opponent injured him would not by itself deny him the use of Res Ipsa Loquitor unless the failure amounts to a knowledge of how the harm was caused and by whom; these are the elements RIL is designed to address in a situation where the defendant is the better party to show what happened.

41. When a legal alien moves into a new state and applies for housing assistance but is refused, the legal alien will not succeed with a court action against the state's decision if:

(A) The legal alien was not entitled to the housing benefits as a matter of local state law applicable to the state's own citizens

(B) The state proves that out of staters are a peculiar source of evil

(C) The Supreme Court has not decided that the fourteenth amendment applies

(D) A well drafted housing law could have erased state discrimination in that state's public housing

Analysis

Consider whether equal protection gives greater rights to a newly arrived resident than it gives to older residents - or the same.
One issue here is equal protection. Note that such assistance as here is not a fundamental right.
Denial will be rationally scrutinized.
Denial of access to housing on the basis of race or national origin would be strictly scrutinized.

42. A party's performance under an impliedin-fact contract is a condition precedent to:
(A) The second party's agreement to perform
(B) The second party's performance
(C) The second party's claim for damages
(D) The first party's entitlement to the second party's expectation

Analysis

The analysis turns on distinguishing (A) from (B) and (B) from (A).
Must one party perform first before the other even agrees to perform?
An implied-in-fact contract is as binding as a

pre-agreed one. It simply forms without preagreement.
If services or goods are received
from a professional, there is an expectancy of
payment.
Ordinarily, there would be an implied
contract for what as been received.
An implied-in-law contract is different. There
is no voluntary acceptance of the service but
the court decrees payment as compensation to
the provider to prevent unjust enrichment and
unjust loss.

43. If a United States citizen who is a woman
acts in concert with a legal alien who is
wealthy in unlawfully killing deer before the
hunting season begins, which of the
following is constitutionally true?

(A) The woman's guilt will be determined
through mid level scrutiny of all the evidence
including evidence of her gender
(B) The woman's guilt and the legal alien's
guilt will be determined through rational
basis scrutiny of all the evidence including
proof of the alien's legal status
(C) The court will not determine the legality
of the hunting law until the appropriate level
of review is determined
(D) The woman's guilt and the legal alien's

guilt will not be a factor in determining whether either is entitled to state-funded representation

Analysis

Laws, regulations, ordinances, other enactments, as well as actions done and judgments rendered on their account, can be constitutionally scrutinized. You must know the different levels of scrutiny - strict, mid level, rationality.

44. During a directors' meeting to approve the sale of all or substantially all of XM corporation's assets to the FM corporation, one of the outside directors present took his own notes so that he could compare them with the official minutes during recess at midday, in order to move a minority motion disapproving the sale.
Which of the following statements is true regarding the admissibility of the director's personally taken notes?

(A) The director's personally taken notes are admissible evidence that he did not vote for the sale
(B) The director's personally taken notes are

admissible evidence that the other directors'
state of mind was to sell
(C) XM corporation can not sell without
majority shareholder approval
(D) This outside director is not an insider of
FM corporation and so has no insider liability
should the sale take place

Analysis

(C) and (D) may or may not be correct under
corporation law but remember that the MBE
does not presently test corporation law.
The best choice turns on whether a person's
notes can be admitted to show not only his
own state of mind but that of another.

Under the rule in Mutual Life Insurance co of
New York et al v Hilmon 145 U.S. 285
(Volume 145 of United States
Reports at page 285) a person's own writings
like a letter can show their own intentions and
be evidence of logically resulting action.

45. The evidence shows that a tax receipt was
sent to Payer by the state tax authorities over
20 years ago. The receipt has been kept in a
locked filing cabinet in Payer's home, a

natural place for it to be kept. It has not been altered and it is not suspicious in appearance. The state is arguing that Payer has not paid proper taxes for the past three years.
Regarding admissibility of the over 20 yearsold tax receipt which of the following is
NOT true?

(A) An ancient document is admissible only if more than 30 years old
(B) The tax receipt sent to Payer by the state tax authorities over 20 years ago is admissible as an ancient document
(C) The tax receipt sent to Payer by the state tax authorities over 20 years ago is relevant to prove Payer's history of tax payments
(D) If not self-authenticating, the tax receipt sent to Payer by the state tax authorities over 20 years ago must be authenticated

Analysis

This question calls for distinguishing the federal ancient document rule from the CA rule.

46. A man went to a US representative's congressional office to get help with finding employment on Capitol Hill.

The congressman promised to personally assist the man with composing a proper political resume.

The man promised in return that if he got hired to a job on Capitol Hill within the next two weeks he would lawfully donate $250 to the congressman's reelection campaign. This agreement is binding on both parties

(A) True
(B) False
(C) Only if the congressman is currently running for reelection
(D) Only if the court finds a contract notwithstanding the laws on official acts

Analysis

Consideration must be bargained for and exchanged. It is questionable whether the congressman's promise induced the promised donation.

But the real issue is whether a congressman can enter into this contract at all.

It is an agreement that may come under a congressman's valid job description (helping citizens find work especially on Capitol Hill) but in return he gets a reelection fund contribution that may or may

not be proper in the circumstances.
The legality of this aspect must be assured
before enforcement can be addressed. Under
contract law if there is illegal consideration there is no
enforceable contract.

47. Involuntary manslaughter is defined in the
jurisdiction as a lesser included offense of
second degree murder. A jury is considering
its verdict on a second degree murder
charge. The jury will be instructed that it may
NOT find involuntary manslaughter on which
of these facts?

(A) Defendant involuntarily fell from a
moving train, landed on a child and killed
him
(B) Defendant while talking on a cell phone
fell from a moving train, landed on a man and
killed him
(C) Defendant while celebrating a betting win
fell from a moving train, landed on a woman
and killed her
(D) Defendant while practicing his martial
arts hobby fell from a moving train, landed on
a police officer and killed him

Analysis

Because involuntary manslaughter is an
unintended killing, it merely requires some unlawful act
(example non-deadly simple battery) or at
least negligence. The right response
will be a situation where there is no intent to
kill but also no qualifying blameworthy act
exists.

48. For eighteen happy years Harry and
Winnie lived in a state with their three
children aged 6, 11 and 17. Just after
Wendy finally succeeded in buying a fuel
efficient electric automobile at a discount
auto auction, they all moved to another state
and bought Green eagles estate, which was
zoned as historic property, for $350,000.
Three years later Harry and Winnie separated
with no intent to reconcile. During property
division the court gave Green eagles estate
and the electric car to Harry and awarded
stocks then worth $300,000 to Winnie.
This property division was agreed between
the parties and their lawyers. The stocks
became worthless almost immediately after
Winnie received them.
Under the US constitution can Winnie reopen
the property division in order to ask for half

of Green eagles?

(A) Yes Winnie may re-open, the constitution does not forbid it
(B) No Winnie may not re-open, the constitution forbids it
(C) Winnie may re-open property division because access to divorce court is fundamental under the due process clause
(D) Yes because Winnie's property has been taken by the state through the court and she must be paid just compensation

Analysis

You should know that access to divorce and divorce court is fundamental for equal protection/due process fundamental rights analysis.
A state can probably declare that any property division is final within reason or that an appeal rather than re-opening is the proper recourse in appropriate cases but the question focuses on the constitutional angle and ignores procedure.

49. Fred validly wrote on a piece of office stationery: "For consideration paid and received, I Fred hereby and by this

deed transfer all my interest in GreenAcre described on the
reverse side, to my friend Robbie." Robbie in fact paid no consideration. Fred has irrevocably delivered the deed to Robbie. Is the deed valid to transfer title?

(A) No consideration was paid - the deed does not transfer vested title
(B) Consideration was not paid but the deed transfers vested title
(C) Consideration was not paid but the deed presently transfers vested title in the future
(D) This form of consideration is arguably incomplete - the deed transfers contingent title

Analysis

A deed will properly transfer property without consideration. For example a land gift will still be given by deed. Vesting relates to whether at the moment the deed is written there is created in the grantee an immediate right to enjoy the property either now or in the future. If there is a future right to enjoy the property the interest is not vested but is either contingent or executory.

50. In an action to recover a hand bag alleged to have been forcibly converted by the defendant, a parking garage, the defendant filed answer to the plaintiff's complaint within the 20 days required by law. The defendant's answer included a counter claim against the plaintiff. The plaintiff failed to file the required reply within the time for filing a reply. The plaintiff was represented by a generally competent attorney. In a malpractice action against the attorney, will the plaintiff prevail?

(A) The plaintiff will prevail if the attorney was not properly licensed in the state where the forcible conversion allegedly took place
(B) The plaintiff will prevail if the attorney cured the defect in the reply within a reasonable time
(C) The plaintiff will recover if the attorney intended to prevail on the colorable merits of the case but failed
(D) The plaintiff will recover if he suffered harm and contributed less than 100% to his harm

Analysis

Conversion is intentional interference with, or a misappropriation of, another's property so severe as to warrant a forced sale to the converter - but you should know that conversion is not the issue here.

Negligence is - did the attorney negligently file late?

If attorney cured the defect in filing within a reasonable time (such that plaintiff suffered no actual harm) then there is little chance of success against him.

You should also consider whether any negligence is shown in (C).

On the California bar examination comparative negligence with joint and several liability holds. A negligence plaintiff will recover only for the injury he didn't do to himself.

However he could claim all damages from one defendant who in many cases then has to pursue his fellow tortfeasors for contribution or indemnity.

Generally there is no contribution from fellow intentional tortfeasors such as fellow trespassers, converters, batterers, or assaulters.

51. In a product liability case the defendant testifies that the alleged defect did not exist at

the time the product left its factory and control. The retailer is then joined in the action. Will the plaintiff recover his cost of purchasing the defective product?

(A) If the jurisdiction awards economic damages, no
(B) If the plaintiff suffered other loss and damage, no
(C) If the jurisdiction recognizes strict product liability, certainly
(D) If the jurisdiction recognizes manufacturer warranty liability, yes

Analysis

The money spent on the defective product is usually treated as economic loss. It can reliably be claimed on a breach of warranty basis. On an essay mention breach of warranty as you discuss strict product liability and explain how rights are affected in jurisdictions A, B and C under the UCC. Otherwise argue that a state 'may' wish to allow economic loss to be recovered in a product liability action, either strict liability or negligent manufacture/ design/labeling/ marketing, although this is not normal.

Nevertheless if there is physical injury or property damage (i.e. damage to property other than the defective product itself) recovery of economic loss is also usually available.

52. In an action to establish the amount of damages for failing to deliver 20 tons of coal to a power plant, Plaintiff claims that the coal mine was negligent in assigning all of its year-to-date production to Disney Worldwide Corp. Defendant denies negligence. The judge rules for Plaintiff on the issue of negligence.

Considering the court's ruling, how will the amount of Plaintiff's contract damages now be calculated?

(A) By proving the monetary difference between the performance the plaintiff received and the performance he expected
(B) By determining money damages for the defendant's negligence
(C) By adding up the difference between the contract and cover price
(D) By adding up the cost of restoring the undelivered coal to the defendant

Analysis

You must know that contract damages include expectation damages, reliance damages, consequential damages and a volume seller's lost profit. Equitable relief like specific performance is available in appropriate cases such as uniqueness or special manufacture. Note that the facts do not say Plaintiff covered for undelivered goods.

53. The police questioned the defendant at his home on suspicion of fraud. The police acted under a valid and properly issued warrant. In an unmarked fraud unit SUV, the defendant was shown a writing. The defendant was asked if he recognized it as a contract he signed a year ago.The defendant did not answer.

The police asked him if he knew a certain man but the defendant did not speak.

Is the defendant entitled to an attorney under the sixth amendment?

(A) No because the right to counsel must be clearly asserted

(B) Yes because a suspect's right to sufficient counsel is constitutionally implied whenever there is custody

(C) No because on the given facts no judicial proceedings appear to have started since the arrest

(D) Yes because a suspect is entitled to an attorney at all stages of a felony prosecution or prosecution for a serious misdemeanor

Analysis

There is no such right as "sufficient counsel." Only if "critical"were added after 'all" would (D) be a proper statement of the law.

54. In deciding a case on certiorari, the US supreme court stated that with certain enumerated exceptions an accused must be allowed family visitation when in custody for more than 30 minutes if the place of custody is more than one mile from his or her residence. Rob has been in custody for two hours in another county and his wife has been with him for one of those hours. The police now want to end Rob's wife's visit.
What is the likely result under this supreme court ruling?

(A) Rob's wife will leave because the police have the same authority to declare an accused's constitutional rights as the supreme court
(B) Rob's wife will leave because the attorney general has the same authority to declare an accused's constitutional rights as the supreme court
(C) Rob's wife will leave and cannot return under the 'No Return' rule
(D) Rob's wife will leave if she is not herself in custody but is probably entitled to return

the next day if Rob is in custody for more
than 30 minutes the next day and the
place of custody is more than one mile from
their home

Analysis

The US supreme court alone determines
constitutional rights. All other organs of
government do not. As the candidate knows,
the rule in option (C) does not exist.

55. During a trial for larceny the jury is given
the following instruction: "The law presumes
that a person intends the consequences of his
act. This presumption can be rebutted. If you
find that the defendant has not rebutted
the presumption that by his acts he intended
to take the property of another, you may but
are not required to, find the defendant
guilty." The jury found the defendant guilty.
Is the defendant entitled to a re-trial?

(A) No because a re-trial constitutes double
jeopardy in violation of the eighth
amendment
(B) No because a re-trial constitutes double
jeopardy in violation of the fifth amendment

(C) No because due process requires that in a criminal case the jury be told that a presumption is binding on it and this jury was not told

(D) Yes because the jury was not told that the defendant must have the intent to permanently deprive the owner of the property and the omission was prejudicial

Analysis

A re-trial does not automatically expose a defendant to 5th amendment double jeopardy. If the offenses are different (one contains an element the other does not) there is no DJ. Moreover a re-trial is allowed after a reversal on appeal, after a hung jury, a remand etc. A presumption is never binding on a criminal jury regarding an element the prosecution must prove beyond a reasonable doubt.

56. In deciding a case on certiorari the supreme court stated that with certain enumerated exceptions an accused must be allowed family visitation when in custody for more than 30 minutes if the place of custody is more than one mile from his or her residence. Dan has been in custody for two days in another state and his wife has

been with him for fifteen minutes on the second day. The police now want to end Dan's wife's visit. What is the likely result?

(A) Dan's wife will leave because the police can determine the length of her visit
(B) Dan's wife will leave because the supreme court has determined the length of her visit
(C) Dan's wife will leave because a local law provides that due process is sufficiently served by the fifteen minutes she has had to visit Dan
(D) Dan's wife will leave because the police have determined that due process is sufficiently served by the fifteen minutes she has had to visit Dan

Analysis

The applicant should be aware that a significant fraction of federal criminal procedure is directed at preventing abuses by police. The candidate must be duly wary of options that increase the power of the police.
Local law can flesh out supreme court rulings where that is the federal/supreme court

intention or there is neither preemption
nor conflict, as with any other federal law.
Here, the court did not stipulate an actual
length of time for visits. Local law can
conceivably do so if based on due
process.

57. For a successful defamation action which
of the following must be FALSE
(A) The evidential statement made by the
defendant
(B) The statement made by the plaintiff
(C) The statement made by the defendant
(D) The statement made by the defendant
negligently, intentionally or with actual
malice if plaintiff is a public
figure

Analysis

A defamation action will not succeed without
proof of the statement's falsity added to
negligence concerning publication at least.
Because of free speech in sone courts
even where the statement is proved false there
must be proof of negligence in not verifying
the truth of what was said.
58.Under the insanity rules a criminal
defendant cannot properly be convicted

unless:

(A) When Defendant shot at Victim, Defendant knew that he was shooting at Victim and that Victim would be hurt or killed

(B) Either the Irresistible impulse test or the M'Naughten test applies

(C) Victim knew the nature and quality of his act

(D) Defendant knew that the Durham insanity test applies

Analysis

Here all the wrong choices are clearly misworded or illogical.

59. If a seller identifies goods that may turn out to be non merchantable, but they have been contracted for sale, there can be no anticipatory repudiation where:

(A) The seller has not shown that he will fail to deliver merchantable goods

(B) Within one month of requesting the insecure party receives assurance of solvency

(C) A merchant's firm offer has been made, which requires no consideration to be binding for 3 months

(D) Cover goods have been pre-purchased and are certain to be delivered

Analysis

The candidate should know the rules on anticipatory repudiation and distinguish it from mere prospective inability to perform.

60. In a criminal trial before a judge sitting without a jury, the defendant on direct examination can introduce evidence to show which of these?

(A) That he suffered from a present sense impression
(B) That the victim did not suffer from a present sense impression
(C) That the defendant is peaceable and law abiding
(D) The internal thought processes of jury members in the jury room

Analysis

Any defendant can lead evidence to show any relevant trait of his character. However, the real issue being tested here is that FRE rules are not different with a jury from without a jury.

61.A valid devise in a will reads: "My farm to
A, my land to C, but if C does not survive me
then my land to to S."
Which of the following statements best
applies to the grant to S?

(A) The gift to S fails because at the moment
of creation it can not be said with certainty
that C will survive the testator
(B) The gift to C is subject to divestment
(C) The gift to A is vested
(D) The gift to S is contingent
The applicant should consider that the
moment A, C and S all die (they are lives in
being at the time the interests were
created), it will be known long before the
additional 21 years whether or not C survived
the testator and so the gift to C is valid under
the rule against perpetuities.

62.The requirement that an accused be
warned of his right to remain silent applies
only when the accused is in custody.
Custody exists where a reasonable person
would realize that he is not free to go. After
three hours of questioning, the police sergeant
has told Fred that he is free to go.

As Fred stands up to leave, another officer who is standing menacingly in the doorway wants to know if Fred has "any place to go." Fred answers no.
The officer arrests Fred under a rarely used criminal homelessness statute.
Can Fred be tried following this arrest?

(A) No because there was no arrest warrant issued
(B) The due process clause applies
(C) Yes because the officer had probable cause
(D) Only if there was no time to obtain an arrest warrant before the arrest could be made

Analysis

An arrest warrant is rarely the issue except for a non exigent   arrest inside a home. Probable cause for the arrest is what's important.
One question here is whether Fred's statement that he has nowhere to go furnishes it because if it does a warrant violation will not bar prosecution.

63. False imprisonment is defined in the jurisdiction as either a wrongful immobilization or the intentional and

unexcused confinement of a person within fixed boundaries against their will. In which of the following situations will the defendant be liable for this tort?

(A) Defendant wanted to lock plaintiff inside a bathroom as a prank

(B) Defendant intended to tie up plaintiff with ropes but did it with a trick towel

(C) Plaintiff demanded that defendant untie her immediately

(D) Plaintiff informed the police that defendant tied her up with strong ropes

Analysis

The statutory definition given here is not substantially different from the one the applicant knows.
An express fact is better than an alleged or implied fact - for example answer (C).

64.The courts of the jurisdiction have consistently ruled that if a trust has real property then forfeitures under the rule against perpetuities may be avoided by making changes to the trust terms.

Which of the following will achieve such changes?

(A) Use cypress to bring the trust terms into compliance with the rule against perpetuities
(B) Increase the period of the rule against perpetuities from 21 years after the death of the last life in being at the time
of the creation of the interest to 30 years or longer
(C) Properly ascertain that the non-trust interests were created when there was a life in being plus twenty one years
(D) Properly ascertain that the trust was created in writing if the jurisdiction requires it

Analysis

Nearly all the choices sound credible. The candidate ought to know how the RAP is defined - and decide which choice allows bad results to be avoided.
RAP definition: An interest must vest if it will vest, within a life in being at its creation plus 21 years. Note that any party or witness to the deed can be such a life.

65. A grantor may lose the power to exercise a right of reentry in which of the

following circumstances?

(A) If the statute of limitations has run
(B) If the rule against perpetuities has been violated
(C) If the property has been destroyed
(D) If the cy press doctrine applies

Analysis

While a right of re-entry is not subject to the RAP as it vests in the grantor from the moment the grantor gives out an interest with a limiting conditionsubsequent like 'but if,' many states do not allow it to hang in the air in perpetuity after it becomes due.

Remember that the holder of the right must actually exercise it unlike a possibility of reverter.

66. John and Tammy receive EuroAcre by deed from John's aunt, Auntie. Auntie wants John and Tammy to have a good start to married life. Auntie is considerably wealthy and very devoted to John. She had previously made a will leaving most of her fortune to him. John knows about the provisions of the

will. He knows that virtually everything
Auntie owns will someday be his. The deed
from auntie was drafted by a prominent
lawyer. It does not specify how John and
Tammy take EuroAcre.
If Tammy rents the part of EuroAcre that she
occupies alone to Start-up, who is Start-up's
landlord?

(A) Tammy because she rented out her
personal space
(B) Auntie, Tammy and John
(C) John because he is Auntie's heir
(D) Tammy and John only

Analysis

The applicant should know that with
exceptions generally having to do with
married couples (example tenancy by the
entirety, community property), profit-sharing
partners and the like, if a deed does not
specify how the takers take, a
tenancy in common is routinely assumed. All
tenants in common are entitled to personally
occupy the entire property not just a portion.
If one tenant rents out rent is owed to all.

67. A man went to a US representative's

congressional office to get help with finding employment on Capitol Hill.

The man obtained his appointment with the congressman through the congressman's reelection campaign staff. The congressman promised to personally assist the man with composing a proper resume. The man thanked the congressman and left. Later that week the man emailed the congressman a promise that if he got hired to a job on Capitol Hill within the next two weeks he would lawfully donate $250 to the congressman's re-election campaign.

Does the man's email provide consideration for the congressman's promise?

(A) Yes

(B) No

(C) Consideration may be either an act or a promise

(D) Consideration must be legally sufficient

Analysis

The applicant must know the rules regarding when consideration is bargained for. A bargain occurs if one promise actually induces the other.

68. Which of these statements qualifies as a

present sense impression?

(A) "I still haven't seen that vintage rifle you bought this morning"
(B) "She believes that's her old bike"
(C) "I remember how mom looked that day"
(D) None of these statements qualifies as a present sense impression

Analysis

FRE Rule 803: Hearsay Exceptions; Availability of Declarant Immaterial.
The following are not excluded by the hearsay rule, even though the declarant is unavailable as a witness:
Presence Sense impression. A statement describing or explaining an event or condition made while the declarant
was perceiving the event or condition, or immediately thereafter.

69. Keith and Karen own 'K House' as joint tenants. Karen borrows $4,000 from I-Credit and I-Credit duly records an interest against 'K House'. The jurisdiction has the following statute:
"Any judgment filed in this state shall, for 8

years from filing, be a lien on the real property then owned or subsequently acquired by any party against whom such a judgment was obtained." What is I-Credit's interest in 'K House' after 'K House' is sold?

(A) I-Credit ceases to have an interest in 'K House' other than in proceeds of the sale
(B) I-Credit is entitled to repossess 'K House' from the buyer in a title theory state
(C) I-Credit is entitled to accelerate repayment by Karen
(D) I-Credit is not entitled to accelerate repayment by Karen

Analysis

(C) may well be true under the loan agreement but tells us nothing about the lender's interest in the disposed collateral under the statute given. The matter to be resolved is whether the statute gives the lender rights to property that the borrower no longer owns - in this lien theory jurisdiction.

70. A man entered a police station and asked to make a domestic complaint against his female partner. The desk officer asked the man to identify himself by showing his driving license. When the man showed the

document the desk officer started to make a photocopy of it. The man objected to this duplication but the desk officer completed photocopying the document.

Two weeks later the man was arrested at his home as a result of information discovered through the use of facts derived from the photocopied driver's license.

The man has brought a federal action alleging that the desk officer, a state actor, had no constitutional grounds to duplicate and store a record of his driver's license. The issue raised by the allegation is:

(A) Unreasonable copying and retention of private drivers license
(B) Unreasonable search (and seizure) of the man's papers and effects
(C) Illegal imprisonment of the man
(D) Illegal larceny of the man's property

Analysis

The rule about a question like this is for an applicant to consider which option is related to the area of law in question. From the interrogatory here, you are dealing with constitutional law. Note that the man was not imprisoned.

71. A man entered a police station and asked to make a domestic complaint against his female partner. The desk officer asked the man to identify himself by showing his driving license. When the man showed the document the desk officer started to make a photocopy of it. The man objected to this duplication but the desk officer completed photocopying the document.

Two weeks later the man was arrested at his home as a result of information discovered through the use of facts derived from the photocopied driver's license. The man has brought a federal action alleging that the desk officer, a state actor, had no constitutional grounds to duplicate and store a record of his driver's license. The desk officer's best defense is that:

(A) The duplication was an administrative search and standardized

(B) The duplication was an administrative search which offered probable cause leading to the later arrest

(C) The search raised reasonable suspicion in the officer's mind

(D) The search was proper as incidental to a valid arrest

Analysis

There was no arrest - the man came in of his own volition to make a complaint. Reasonable suspicion cannot lead to a search but only to a stop. Fear for the officer's safety will then allow for a frisk of outer clothing for weapons. Only probable cause will justify a search. If instead it is a search which leads to probable cause, there is a problem. The evidence obtained will be tainted.

72. While flying overhead in a helicopter, the police saw a man taking a bath out of a bucket in the open air. They arrested the man on a misdemeanor charge. During a search of the area the man around the man after he had dressed, the police discovered contraband. He was taken to his home where more contraband was found in a large closet. Further investigation showed that the man was the leader of an extensive illegal importation ring.
Can the man get the contraband found at his home suppressed?

(A) No, validly discovered evidence cannot be suppressed
(B) No, validly seized contraband cannot be suppressed

(C) Chances are good, the search of his home required probable cause

(D) No, the search of his home required reasonable suspicion

Analysis

See Mcdonald V. United States, 335 U.S. 451

73. A man entered a police station and asked to make a domestic complaint against his female partner. The desk officer asked the man to identify himself by showing his driving license. When the man showed the document the desk officer started to make a photocopy of it.

The man objected to this duplication but the desk officer completed photocopying the document. Two weeks later the man was arrested at his home as a result of information discovered through the use of facts derived from the photocopied driver's license. The man has brought a federal action alleging that the desk officer, a state actor, had no constitutional grounds to duplicate and store a record of his driver's license.

Can the man successfully keep evidence of his being the leader of an illegal importation ring from the jury?

(A) No, because the search that led to the discovery was valid

(B) No, because the seizure of the license was also a search

(C) No, because an accused cannot have evidence against him suppressed at his own trial

(D) No, because the writ of mandate is available to quash any wrongful conviction of the defendant on appeal

Analysis

On an essay, the state is going to say that the search was administrative and standardized: it is true that photocopying the license for storage is an invasion of privacy but at the very least the police need the documentation for their records. They will argue that the copying and filing are a necessary official inventory.

Moreover, a court may conclude that a person voluntarily entering the ream of the police to make a report would expect such privacydiminishing official measures.

On an essay argue whether all this justifies actual use of the information in actual crimefighting.

74. A jurisdiction defines embezzlement to

include theft of electricity services. A homeowner paid an electrician to connect her property back to the public grid after the home owner's property was removed from the public grid by the electric company for non-payment. If the homeowner is prosecuted for embezzlement, will the prosecution succeed?

(A) Yes because the homeowner paid the electrician to do an illegal act

(B) No because the homeowner had no right to the reconnected electricity

(C) Yes because the electricity was wrongfully taken with intent to deprive the electric company of it

(D) Yes because the electricity was the property of another

Analysis

For embezzlement the property of another alleged to be stolen must have initially been in the lawful possession of the accused (more than mere custody) before the intent to permanently deprive the owner of it formed, followed by unlawful deprivation of the (owner.) The candidate should consider that the misappropriated electricity was not in the proper lawful possession of the accused and there was larceny only.

75. In a tort action between Al and Bath, evidence has been presented showing that during a fight in a downtown bar,
Bath kicked Al and Al punched Bath. Two days later, a paralegal wrote to Al on behalf of Bath, in criminal violation of the state's laws forbidding the unauthorized practice of law. The letter said that Bath attacked Al but claimed that Al then escalated the violence.
Will the court admit the illegally written letter in evidence?

(A) Yes, as an adoptive party admission
(B) Yes, as a hearsay exemption
(C) Yes, as a hearsay exception
(D) No, because the para-legal illegally acted as counsel

Analysis

Note that under the FRE an admission does not have to be authorized. At common law it was and under Ca's CEC it is.

76. Buy emailed Sell a request for a price range for various models of decorative plastic fruit. Sell's reply listed prices for decorative plastic animals. Without realizing this, Buy ordered 500 premium items which were delivered to Sell the day after the order was placed. Buy refuses to pay for the plastic animals. Sell offers 'to tear up our contract' and replace the plastic animals with plastic fruit at the right price and Buy agrees. However Buy refuses to pay shipping costs to return the rejected plastic animals to Sell.
Is Sell obligated to pay the cost of shipping the rejected animals?

(A) Yes because Sell impliedly agreed to pay the cost when the original contract was mutually rescinded
(B) No because there was no UCC consideration for the modification on Buy's part
(C) Yes because they are Sell's property
(D) No because Buy was in breach of the original contract

Analysis

There is no 'UCC consideration' for a

modification. Under (C), the goods are Sell's property only before any contract
for their sale, and before any identification to any such contract.

The original contract was breached if Buy's mistake was unilateral, making him liable to take due care of the goods and hold/return them at the Seller's word - but then that contract with all its mistakes was mutually rescinded.

Although there is an issue around rescinding an already performed contract, that was the intent of the parties because of mutual mistakes. They agreed to 'tear up' their contract.

Restitution then follows.

Restitution at law (by right) or a equity (to prevent injustice/unjust enrichment) usually returns the parties to their re-contract positions, meaning that Sell gets the goods back but Buy expends no money - equal to Sell paying for the return. Or a split.

The above is only one possible line of thought but the chosen answer is the best of the alternatives given.

77. Congress passes a law providing in part: "Subject to the fines hereunder prescribed, no person driving a motor vehicle on a federal

road after nightfall may use headlight
high beams unless the car is over ten years
old and visibility would be seriously impaired
without high beams." Other than the
commerce clause, the best constitutional
ground for passing this law is:

(A) The dormant commerce clause
(B) The federal police power as limited by the
tenth amendment
(C) The federal power to levy and collect
taxes
(D) The federal power to regulate national
health and safety

Analysis

The federal power in the last choice doesn't
exist nor does the one in the second option.
The DCC forbids states from
making laws that burden or discriminate
against inter state commerce unless there is
no other way to address the problem for the
acting state's benefit. There is a federal
power to tax (and to spend but only for the
general welfare.)

78.A man went to a private tax preparation
office to have his returns prepared and

electronically filed. The first
employee took the man's information,
including the man's alien registration number.
That employee passed the man's
file to her colleague, a tax analyst.
The tax analyst explained the effects of the
current rules on the man's tax liability. He
then passed the man and his file to another
employee who confirmed what the
analyst said.
This third employee sent the man's tax return
to the tax authority electronically in the man's
presence.
Eight months later the tax authorities sued the
man for a tax deficiency. The man believes
that 'somebody' at the tax preparation
company 'did not do their job.' The
man cannot prove who proximately caused
his harm.
Which of the following statements is true?

(A) The tax preparation company proximately
caused the man's harm
(B) The tax preparation company is the cause
in fact of the man's harm
(C) The man does not have to identify which
particular worker directly caused his harm
(D) The man has to show the exact extent of
damage he has suffered

Analysis

The final option is not related to proximate cause but to accurate proof of damages. A dictionary defines proximate as Very near or Next, as in space, time, or order.
The first option is conclusory while the one following it is related to actual cause and not proximate cause.
Res ipsa loquitur gets a case to the jury where the plaintiff has no way to show how a number of potential feasors (or one) behaved when the injury occurred.

79. Tess bought an airline ticket intending to fly out to a class reunion in another city on Thursday. A term of the sale was that for an additional sum which she paid, the purchased ticket became transferrable to another traveller.
On Wednesday Tess decided that her bedridden mother could not be left alone. She sold the airline ticket to Pati. When Pati attempted to board the flight she was refused boarding. Pati and Tess have sued the airline for breach of contract.
Which of the following statements is NOT true?

(A) The airline had no duty to board Pati
(B) The airline entered into an agreement
with Tess
(C) The airline has no rights to the money
paid to Tess by Pati
(D) The airline has a right to refuse to board
Pati for safety reasons

Analysis

Tess entered into a contract with the airline.
The terms included transferability of the
ticket she purchased under
that contract. The issue is whether the airline
must honor the mutual agreement when its
performance time arrives.

80. A federal civil servant's truck was searched while properly parked in the employee parking lot. The federal civil servant made objections to the search. It was conducted by federal security agents acting on a reliable tip off. Stolen jewelry was found in the federal civil servant's truck. At his trial the federal civil servant seeks to have the jewelry excluded from evidence. Will he succeed?

(A) No, the search was legal

(B) No, the search was reasonable

(C) No, the tip-off provided probable cause for the search

(D) No, the police did not conduct the search

Analysis

For constitutional actions there must be government action except under the 13th amendment.

Federal criminal procedure could be thought of as the criminal law arm of constitutional law.

Its rules must accord with constitutional guarantees and freedoms: such things as state action, privacy, reasonableness, probable cause, reasonable suspicion, voluntariness of confessions, and warrants are its concerns.

81. A college student needed money. She asked another college student if the other student would help in a gas station robbery, explaining that the gas station was too large to be robbed by one person. The second college student agreed to the plan, not knowing that the first college student had no intention of carrying it out. If both college students are charged with conspiracy to commit robbery, will the prosecution succeed in a modern jurisdiction?

(A) The students reached agreement; the prosecution will succeed
(B) The students reached agreement but intent to do the crime is necessary; at worst prosecution of only the second student will succeed
(c) The first student solicited the second student; prosecution for solicitation will succeed
(D) The second student has committed no solicitation

Analysis

Without mens rea there is no crime except for strict liability violations like traffic offenses. Common law conspiracy requires an agreement (implied by actions or expressly communicated) to commit a crime or to do a lawful act by unlawful means. Modernly an overt act is required.

However, modern conspiracy is a specific intent crime, not a general intent crime. This means that more than an agreement to commit the crime is needed. An intent to commit it is also generally required. This intent may be shown circumstantially by an overt act.

The candidate must at all times distinguish attempt (elements are intent, substantial step) from conspiracy (elements are agreement, modernly overt act).

82. In July, Jed, the owner of a profitable fish pond, sold it to a high-end restaurant for $130,000. In August another restaurant developed an interest in the fish pond and opened negotiations to buy it. Also in August Jed gave a properly signed deed to his doctor as part payment for extensive medical treatment.

What is the state of title to the fish pond?

(A) It depends on the jurisdiction's recording laws

(B) If the deed to the doctor affects the fish pond it depends on the jurisdiction's recording laws

(C) The state of the title is unchanged

(D) The state of the title has changed

Analysis

Two factors have the potential to affect the title received by the high-end restaurant. They are the deed to the doctor - did it grant the same land to another? And, what do the recording laws say about whatever order the grantees recorded their interests in?

83. The state has passed a new law which provides in part:

"It shall be a misdemeanor punishable by a fine not to exceed $200 for a first or second offense for any person to denounce the United States, if the denunciation is published to at least two persons separately or together."

Speaker plans to make a speech on a public beach on the 4th of July to whoever will listen, declaring that the United States is "disunited and in no state."

Speaker does not know that because of riots

in the past, a license is required for a speech on the beach unless the speech it is a commercial advertisement. In view of the new law, will Speaker have to obtain a license before his speech on the 4th of July?

(A) The law is vague on its face - no
(B) The law burdens the freedom of speech - no
(C) The law does not provide for a judicial by-pass - no
(D) The law does not represent supreme court rulings on speech and debate - no

Analysis

The task here is to determine whether there is sufficient clarity in a law that punishes one if they 'denounce' the US.
See for example Papachristou v. City of Jacksonville, 405 U.S. 156 1972.
84. Defendant is on trial for abducting a child who was on her way to school. Defendant's lawyer presents a witness who says that the defendant has a reputation for being law abiding and a friendly neighbor. The state seeks to introduce witness' arrest record for theft. Can the state introduce this evidence?

(A) Only if the witness first credibly admits the arrests

(B) The state can introduce this evidence on cross examination

(C) Only if the evidence is not related to a conviction

(D) Only if the evidence is related to misconduct

Analysis

FRE 608 Specific Instances of Conduct.
Except for a criminal conviction under Rule 609, extrinsic evidence is not admissible to prove specific instances of a witness's conduct in order to attack or support the witness's character for truthfulness.
But the court may, on cross-examination, allow them to be inquired into if they are probative of the character for truthfulness or untruthfulness of (1) the witness; or (2) another witness whose character the witness being cross examined has testified about.

Rule 405
(a) By Reputation or Opinion. When evidence of a person's character or character trait is admissible, it may be proved by testimony about the person's reputation or by testimony

in the form of an opinion.

On cross-examination of the character witness, the court may allow an inquiry into relevant specific instances of the person's conduct.

(b) By Specific Instances of Conduct. When a person's character or character trait is an essential element of a charge, claim, or defense, the character or trait may also be proved by relevant specific instances of the person's conduct.

85. The best claim fifteen year old Piper can bring against a teacher who called her fatty is

(A) A claim for official infliction of emotional distress
(B) A claim for negligent breach of teacher's duty resulting in physical harm
(C) A claim for intentional infliction of emotional distress
(D) A claim for verbal assault and battery resulting in depression

Analysis

This kind of question and this array of choices, is a giveaway on the examination. An applicant should be careful to collect all give-away points available. The best value of the MBE portion is that a high score can successfully offset points lost in the written portion.

86. Father devises property "to A and B as tenants in common, A to own a 2/3 share and B a 1/3 share." B rents the property to a tenant and collects the rent. Which of the following is true?

(A) A must remove B from the property by eviction but not by foreclosure
(B) B must account to A and B for the rent received
(C) Since B is entitled to occupy the entire property no accounting is necessary until partition by sale.
(D) A must occupy 2/3 of the property and B only 1/3

Analysis

The applicant must remember generally that
tenants in common share and own everything
equally until the moment of partition.
Only then does it matter who holds in what
lesser or greater share - the property or sale
proceeds will be divided in that proportion.
However, occupation through a tenant raises
equality issues.

87. A man refuses to rent his store to the Red
cross, stating that the Red Cross is a racist
organization.
Which relief is constitutionally barred?

(A) Damages for violating the due process
rights of the Red Cross
(B) Damages for breach of contract
(C) Revocation of the contract with the man
(D) Damages for defamation on proof that the
man knowingly damaged the character of the
Red Cross

Analysis

Although the candidate must know the
categories of unprotected speech, e.g.
defamation, they are not relevant to

answering this question because a starting threshold is not met: the facts do not show that the Red Cross is a state actor.

88. The President of Acme corporation takes a tea bag out of a box in the executive lounge for use but forgets it in a tea cup. Because he did not properly close the box, all the tea bags go bad.
A company executive makes a cup of tea with one these bad tea bags and falls ill. Other than negligence, what could the executive sue the President for?

(A) Negligence
(B) Battery
(C) Assault
(D) Larceny or embezzlement of company property

Analysis

A tortious battery is the intentional causing of a harmful or offensive bodily contact. In a debatable case an awareness
of substantial certainty of contact can suffice for intent.
Here, was it substantially certain that

someone would suffer unpleasant contact with the bad tea bags?
Remember that a criminal battery cannot be 'sued' upon but only prosecuted by the state.

89. Dog trainer is a nationally renowned trainer of 'intelligent dogs.' Dog trainer disputes a boundary with a woman. Dog trainer commands one of his trainee dogs to go into the woman's home, find her property deed, and bring it to Dog trainer. The dog obeys.
With what crimes can Dog trainer be charged?

(A) Larceny
(B) Invasion of privacy
(C) Conversion
(D) A strict liability crime

Analysis

(B)and (C) are not tested on the MBE as crimes. Can a crime be committed through an agent?

90. Services advertised a sale on KTY radio. The sale was to begin at 11pm on Black friday. The KTY program announcer said, "This will be the mother of

all sales! New homes at half price!" This was
the announcer's error as Services owned a
chain of grocery stores and sold no
homes.
What was Services' duty to a woman who
arrived at the sale expecting to buy a half-priced
home and was trampled?

(A) To make the premises safe
(B) To inspect for hidden dangers
(C) To control the crowd safely
(D) All of the above

Analysis

Ordinarily the operator of a business premises
owes an invitee all the duties mentioned. The
troubling issue is whether the candidate
should restrict her answer to (C)
since it is the most relevant to what happened
to this particular invitee on this particular
occasion.
The answer is: No. Because the trampled
woman was owed all duties owed to a
business invitee - not just the one actually
breached.

91. Services advertised a sale on KTY radio.
The sale was to begin at 11pm on Black

friday. The KTY program announcer said, "This will be the mother of all sales! New homes at half price!" This was the announcer's error as Services owed a chain of grocery stores and sold no cars. Can the program announcer's statement be admitted in an action to determine Services' liability to a woman who arrives at the sale expecting to buy a half-priced home but is disappointed?

(A) Yes, under the state of mind exclusion subject to authentication, logical and legal relevancy
(B) Yes, it is a party admission by Services as a corporate speaker
(C) Yes, for its effect on the woman
(D) Yes, under the hear-say exception

Analysis

The TV station's program announcer is not shown to be speaking for Services at all nor to be under its control and cannot make an admission for Services nor show its state of mind on any matter.

92. In a common law jurisdiction arson cannot be committed

(A) Without an accomplice
(B) At night
(C) Without malice
(D) In the day

Analysis

Common law arson involves the malicious burning of the dwelling of another. A modern statute may expand this definition.
The interrogatory specifies common law.

93. Painter contracted to paint a private zoo for $54,000. The question before the court is whether the contract called for acme paint or rotor paint. Under the UCC the court can:

(A) Rely on the common law
(B) Admit no expert opinion
(C) Take judicial notice
(D) Recuse itself under UCC Section 2-202

Analysis

S 2-202 is not relevant.

It says that agreed or written terms intended to be final expressions cannot be not be contradicted by evidence of any previous oral or written agreement but can however be explained or supplemented a by course of dealing or usage of trade or by course of performance.

Also by evidence of consistent additional terms. But not even consistent additional terms allowed where the court deems the writing to be a complete integration.

The candidate may want to consider S 1-103 instead. It says that common law and equity, the law merchant, common law regarding capacity to contract, the law of principal and agent, of estoppel, fraud, misrepresentation, duress, coercion, mistake, Bankruptcy, or other validating or invalidating cause - can supplement the UCC.

94. Congress has passed a law taking away the President's power to "declare war on terrorist organizations and individuals." The President and the Department of Justice ('DOJ') object to the new law and file suit in Federal court. If the court declines to hear the matter it will likely be because

(A) The power to declare war is conferred on

congress and the power to wage war on the President

(B) There is no diversity of citizenship between the President, the DOJ on one hand and the congress on the other

(C) There is no amount in controversy and if there is, it is less than $75,000

(D) The federal court judge is new and inexperienced

Analysis

Option (D) may well be true but is not a response to even briefly consider on an examination. Amount in controversy applies to diversity actions only not federal question cases lie this. Same for diversity of citizenship. Civil Pro is not tested per se on the California MBE.

The President et al v Congress would raise a federal question and would not need to fulfill any of the requirements of diversity jurisdiction.

But one ground for lack of justiciability is that the question raised is political. Political questions involve issues that the court decides are to be decided not by itself but by another branch of government. There are few of these.

95. Anthony is stopped by four patrolling private security guards on his way to his sister's wedding, asked to exit his vehicle and frisked on suspicion of being armed. Two of the security guards are extremely menacing and at one stage threaten to shoot him dead. Anthony is a United States citizen with no criminal record. What are his constitutional claims and against whom?

(A) On the facts no constitutional claims lie against anybody
Analysis: Because there has been no action by a state actor.
(B) First amendment claims against the state
(C) Fourth and first amendment claims against the guards
(D) Fifth and fourth amendment claims against the state and the employer of the guards

96. Thea agreed with Lloyd to live in Lloyd's basement for the four months before her medical school finals. She agreed to pay $500 to Lloyd before she moved out. In an action between the parties, Thea moves for summary judgment on the grounds that no facts establish a tenancy.

The motion is denied because:

(A) A tenancy for years existed
(B) A periodic tenancy existed
(C) A tenancy at will existed
(D) A tenancy at sufferance existed

Analysis

A tenancy for years is created for a fixed number of years but can be for a fixed fraction of a year such as three months.
A periodic tenancy goes on from period to period automatically until one party gives notice to end it.
A tenancy at will is often non transferable and gives the agreed right to occupy and quit at any time without pre agreeing to a length of occupation. However states impose a requirement of notice, usually 30 days.
A tenancy at sufferance involves a hold-over tenant who stays on after a lease has ended until the landlord demands the premises back. The hold over tenant is bound by the terms of his expired lease such as the rent amount and due date.

A tenancy at sufferance differs from a

tenancy at will in that there is no agreement creating a tenancy at sufferance because it arises automatically when the tenant does not vacate.

97. In a contract-related action between Supplier ('S'), a citizen of state X, and Manufacturer ('M'), incorporated in state Y, which of the following pieces of evidence will NOT be admitted in federal court and why not?

(A) An admission by S that S did not supply the right quantity of goods, because S did supply the right quantity of goods Admissible as an admission

(B) An admission by M that M did not pay for supplies made by S, because M did pay for supplies made by S Admissible as an admission

(C) A written warehouse record prepared by M's workers showing that no record of receipt of any goods sent by M was ever made Admissible as a business record

(D) A signed Fedex receipt showing that goods were received by M, because it is not shown that it was S who sent the goods received Not Admissible.

Not authenticated

Analysis

A party admission is always admissible however foolish, untrue or unwise, even if it fulfills the restrictions on hear say. It is just never hearsay under the federal rules. Note that the term includes any statement made out of court by a party or her representative (in Ca authorized only) even if not an 'admission' in the lay sense.
Example: it is a party admission if one party says 'It rained on Tuesday." If it's relevant it will go not the evidence.

Absence of an entry in an authenticated business or public record will be admissible to show that an event which
would have been recorded did not occur. Recall that entries in such records must be made by or from information supplied by one with personal knowledge and close in time to the event. But such an entry must still help to logically prove or help to logically disprove some fact. (CA - in dispute.)

Illustration; an accurate record that in Eastern San Diego at 9:21AM on March the 26th, the ground was wet with snow would not help to logically prove or disprove an issue that of whether cancer causes death.

98. Defendant is on trial for murder with a deadly weapon.
The prosecution proposes to introduce evidence that on the day of the victim's death Defendant purchased a gun and ammunition. Will Defendant be allowed to call a witness to show Defendant's reputation for organizing four antigun protest marches in the last four years?

(A) Yes because it proves that the defendant did not commit the crime
(B) Yes because it is habit evidence
(C) Yes because of the preponderance of evidence of the marches
(D) Yes because the defendant is entitled to present evidence of a pertinent character trait

Analysis

In CA always remember prop 8.
FRE Rule 404
(a) Character Evidence.
(1) Prohibited Uses. Evidence of a person's character or character trait is not admissible

to prove that on a particular occasion the person acted in accordance with the character or trait.

(2) Exceptions for a Defendant or Victim in a Criminal Case.
The following exceptions apply in a criminal case:

(A) a defendant may offer evidence of the defendant's pertinent trait, and if the evidence is admitted, the prosecutor may offer evidence to rebut it;

(B) subject to the limitations in Rule 412, a defendant may offer evidence of an alleged victim's pertinent trait, and if the evidence is admitted, the prosecutor may:
(i) offer evidence to rebut it; and
(ii) offer evidence of the defendant's same trait; and

(C) in a homicide case, the prosecutor may offer evidence of the alleged victim's trait of peacefulness to rebut evidence that the victim was the first aggressor.

(3) Exceptions for a Witness. Evidence of a witness's character may be admitted under Rules 607, 608, and 609.

(b) Crimes, Wrongs, or Other Acts.
(1) Prohibited Uses.

Evidence of a crime, wrong, or other act is not admissible to prove a person's character in order to show that on a particular occasion the person acted in accordance with the character.

(2) Permitted Uses; Notice in a Criminal Case.
This evidence may be admissible for another purpose, such as proving motive, opportunity, intent, preparation, plan, knowledge, identity, absence of mistake, or lack of accident.
On request by a defendant in a criminal case, the prosecutor must:

(A) provide reasonable notice of the general nature of any such evidence that the prosecutor intends to offer at trial; and
(B) do so before trial — or during trial if the court, for good cause, excuses lack of pretrial notice.

99a. By warranty deed, owner sold a developed parcel of land to Buyer. Fourteen years later Buyer found a demand to vacate the premises in his mail. It came from the tax authorities. The demand stated that on the date owner sold the land, owner was indebted for tax and that by law the tax authorities had a lien on the property. Buyer does not believe that a lien authorizes the tax authorities to demand that he vacate the property.

Buyer contacts owner because:

(A) Owner conveyed to him by warranty deed
(B) Owner conveyed to him by quit claim deed
(C) Owner breached the covenant of seising
(D) Owner breached the covenant of right to convey

Analysis

The covenant of right to convey, the covenant of seising and the covenant against undisclosed encumbrances are not the same things. This rules out both (C) and (D).
A general warranty deed does make the present covenants of seisin and right to convey, telling the buyer or other

grantee that the seller has title and right to sell or otherwise convey. It also makes a covenant against undisclosed encumbrances.

Two future covenants in a general warranty do insulate the grantee from future claims of better (paramount) title by anyone - the covenant of quiet enjoyment and the ambiguously named 'covenant of warranty.' The covenant of further assurances does undertake to take any further steps necessary to perfect grantee's title whenever the need arises. For example if some document was once misfiled by the grantor and this is affecting grantee's title, the grantor undertakes to correct the situation or its effects.

99b. State X has banned the importation of nuclear waste from state Y. In retaliation, state Y has banned the exportation of nuclear waste from state X into state Y. In an action between a nuclear plant operator on the one hand and both state X and state Y on the other:

(A) The nuclear plant operator has standing because it operates several nuclear power plants in state Y

(B) The nuclear plant operator has standing:

inter state production is burdened by being no longer able to export industrial material

(C) The nuclear plant operator has standing: it operates a nuclear power plant in state X and has done so for many years with millions of innocent customers heavily depending on it

(D) The nuclear plant operator has no standing because its plants in state Y produce gaseous pollution and petroleum debris but no nuclear waste

Analysis

One basic issue affecting standing in constitutional law - whether under the commerce clause or the dormant commerce clause or some other constitutional rule - is whether the plaintiff has suffered an individuated injury in- fact caused by the particular defendant and which will be relieved by the court's decision.

100. Pilot is employed by a charter airline to fly a minimum of three thousand miles each month. The pilot belongs to Trade Association. The Daily News publishes a list of Trade Association members who fly "three thousand dangerous miles each month."

Pilot brings a False Light action daily News. What is the likely result?

(A) Daily News will win because Trade Association is newsworthy

(B) Pilot will win because Daily News published the false
story about Trade Association members

(C) Daily News will win because it is a news organization

(D) Pilot will win because Daily News created a false impression that Pilot is engaging in dangerous flight

Analysis

False light alleges that defendant created of a false impression that would be highly offensive to a reasonable person. That is - it's reasonable for plaintiff to be highly offended. See Gill v. Curtis Publishing Co. 239 P.2d 630 (Cal. 1952) for general understanding.

Note: Not all states recognize the tort. For this question consider first amendment privileges of the press.

Value Bar Prep bonus question

Which two elements must be proved to show a fifth amendment due process violation?

(A) Federal action, no viable defense
(B) Federal action, no compelling government objective
(C) Federal action, uncompensated taking
(D) Federal action, no legitimate government objective

Analysis

The fifth amendment due process clause is the federal equivalent of the 14th amendment due process responsibility of states. 1t makes the federals subject to the constitution.
The Takings clause is a 5th amendment issue that applies to a state or local government as well as the federal government.

Value Bar Prep bonus question

Why did Dora fail to win a privacy action after Peter watched her while she undressed?

(A) Dora did not protest

(B) Dora's window was wide open

(C) Dora knew Peter

(D) Peter had seen her undress many times before

Analysis

The privacy right protects the right to privacy - the right to be left alone - only when the expectation of privacy is reasonable.

Californiabarhelp.com

Click on us for bar prep or baby bar prep. We wrote 6 Model bar essays and 2 Model performance tests.

Made in the USA
San Bernardino, CA
04 February 2018